Ricky Elliott

The Quintet Chorus - A Woodland Adventure

Nightingale Books

NIGHTINGALE PAPERBACK

© Copyright 2025 Ricky Elliott

The right of Ricky Elliott to be identified as author of
this work has been asserted by him in accordance with the
Copyright, Designs and Patents Act 1988.

All Rights Reserved

No reproduction, copy or transmission of this publication
may be made without written permission.
No paragraph of this publication may be reproduced,
copied or transmitted save with the written permission of the publisher, or in accordance
with the provisions of the Copyright Act 1956 (as amended).

Any person who commits any unauthorised act in relation to
this publication may be liable to criminal prosecution and civil claims for damages.

A CIP catalogue record for this title is available from the British Library.
ISBN 978 1 78788 348 2

Nightingale Books is an imprint of
Pegasus Elliot MacKenzie Publishers Ltd.
www.pegasuspublishers.com

First Published in 2025

Nightingale Books
Sheraton House Castle Park
Cambridge England

Printed & Bound in Great Britain

Dedication

To Fay (my Mother) for giving me the inspiration and belief.

In a magical kingdom in a land not far away from you is a village called Willowdown. Near the village is Willow Wood, which has five pathways called a 'quintet' leading to an oak tree which had been standing in the Wood for over three hundred years. Inside the old oak tree is a group of birds affectionately known as the 'Quintet Chorus'. Every Tuesday morning, they would gather together to sing songs and recite poetry of times long ago. The chorus was made up of the following tuneful birds: Suki Sparrow and her team of five Sparrowettes, named after the five pathways to the tree; Tommy Thrush, Ricky Robin, Babs Blackbird, Wendy Wagtail, Roger Rook and Paula Pigeon.

Leading the choir was their choirmaster, Ollie Owl, known as the 'Wise One'. He had lived in the Wood for many years and had seen birds, young and old, come and go. As the chorus were joyfully singing the words to 'All Birds Wise and Wonderful' a figure appeared in the doorway to the tree. It was their security chief, Harry Hawk, who led his Hawker Squadron in protecting the Wood from poachers, litterbugs and unwelcome visitors.

"I've just flown through the town of Wendlebury," he said, "and happened to notice

Wally Wendover, the CEO of Build 'em High Construction, entering the Town Hall for a meeting with the mayor. How did I know this? Well, I perched on the ledge outside the mayor's office and the window happened to be open, so I could hear every word they were saying."

"Is this going to be another of your long-drawn-out stories that doesn't have an ending or, in most cases, a beginning?" remarked Suki.

"Now, young Sparrow," barked Ollie, "please behave and listen to what Harry has to say."

"Well," said Harry, "I think we could be in a lot of danger. Wally wasn't meeting the mayor, Peter Proctor, but his deputy, Danny 'the Dodgeball' Green. Wally was showing 'the Dodgeball' plans for a large housing estate and shopping centre where our Wood is now. Work will start on Thursday morning and Wendover has been given a large amount of money to get the work done as quickly as possible."

Ricky Robin interrupted the conversation and asked, "Does the mayor know anything about this?"

"No," said Harry, "as he is currently on sick leave and won't be back for a while."

Suddenly a large rumbling sound was heard nearby. Babs looked at the assembled group and said, "I hate to break up the fun, but diggers can be seen coming into the village heading this way. They are about a mile away."

"This can't be right," said Ollie. "It's not even Thursday yet and the Wood is protected by a decree laid down by the Order of the Golden Swan and the Palace of the Cygnets. I've got a copy of the paper here in the book on the History of the Chorus, which says that nothing can be built in our woods ever!"

"OK, we haven't got long," said Ollie. "No more singing today, as a plan of action needs to be drawn up right now. Ricky, go down to the Royal Jelly Hives and tell Billy Bumble what is happening and bring along the Queen Bee and her hive ready for action. Suki, take your Sparrowettes and change all the road signs leading into the wood. Tommy, Babs, Wendy, Roger and Paula, get down to the construction vehicles and in the words of my old grandfather, 'knobble 'em'. Some 'umans (human beings) think that the woodland and its inhabitants can make way for cheap housing and poor-quality shops. They're wrong! The Quintet Chorus are here to stay!

Harry, take your squadron to the council offices and bring back the money and illegal documents, including the plans, as quickly as possible."

In the blink of an eye, a plan of action was underway. As they left the tree, one of Harry's young hawks, Barney, entered and said to Ollie, "The mayor, Peter Proctor, is on his way back to work."

"How do you know this?" queried Ollie.

"Well, I went along with Harry to the council offices today and stayed behind on the window ledge. His secretary had come back into his room and had taken a phone call from him."

Ollie moved closer to Barney and said, "You need to catch up with the Hawker Squadron, get the money and plans and bring them back to the wood. Although we don't mix with the 'umans (human beings), the mayor needs to be aware of what's going on. Barney, catch up with Harry, tell him the news and take everything away before the mayor arrives back."

"Yes, Ollie, I will," said Barney and left the tree hastily.

Meanwhile, on the outskirts of the village, Suki and the Sparrowettes were changing the signs to the wood.

"Now listen, girls," said Suki. "We need to make sure that these builders get nowhere near this Wood or even its fringes. If this works, the signs will lead them from the Wood into the old smelly bog."

Within minutes, Danny 'the Dodgeball' Green and Wally Wendover were leading the construction vehicles towards the edge of Willow Wood.

"There we go, Danny," Wally said. "The sign says we must take a left here, which leads into the Wood."

However, they were both unaware that Suki and her Sparrowettes were hiding behind a group of trees situated on the woodland's edge. "Right, girls, we'll wait here until the rest of the gang turns up."

Five minutes later, there was chaos as the signs had led Danny and Wally into the swampy bog. The plan had worked! The other workers' vehicles were stuck in the foul-smelling bog and they were falling out of them into the gooey stench, stuck upright like muddy statues.

"What's happened here?" Danny enquired. "We've been led down the wrong road!"

As Danny said this, Billy Bumble, the Queen Bee and her hive of bees dived down into the group of builders and contractors, giving them a royal jelly surprise! Bee stings on their faces, hands and legs.

"Back up," said Danny. "Let's get out of here!"

As Danny said this, Tommy, Babs, Wendy, Roger and Paula flew in and started removing the valves from their vehicles' tyres. With a hiss and a burp, the tyres quickly went down.

"Danny, what's going on here?" queried Wally. "I thought everything was going to be okay with this building project?"

"Run," said Danny. "We can't stay around here as we don't have permission to build on this site."

As he said this, Peter Proctor, the mayor, roared up on his large Darley Havison motorbike. "What do you think you are doing, Dodgeball?"

"Nothing, boss," said Danny. "I was just looking at this new equipment that our council could use."

"You're lying," said the mayor. "You're up to something, I know!"

Just as the mayor said this, a loud bang was heard overhead and two bin liners full of cash and illegal papers landed at the mayor's feet, including a copy of the Golden Swan decree.

The mayor jumped with surprise and then started to carefully look through the two bin liners. Harry, Barney and the Hawker Squadron had completed their mission by returning to the council offices to collect the evidence.

"You've lied and cheated your way into this job, Dodgeball," said the mayor, holding up the illegal contract in his hand. "And you, Wendover, and the rest of your dodgy idiots will never work again. Jail sentences for the lot of you!"

The mayor pulled his mobile phone from his leather biker jacket and rang the police. As the police arrived to arrest the two men and the boggy builders, the birds and the hive bees, including Billy and the Queen, gathered together out of sight of the 'umans (human beings), pleased that their job was done.

An hour later, Ollie had gathered all the birds in a line on one of the five pathways leading to the oak tree, thanking them all for their hard work.

"Youngsters of the wood, for your bravery today, I am awarding you the highest honour from the Order of the Golden Swan."

Ollie then pinned medals onto their proud chests, which featured a Golden Swan with its wings outstretched and below it were the words 'For Bravery'.

"This is a royal wood and environmentally friendly," continued Ollie, "and no buildings of any kind will ever destroy the natural beauty and nature in our wood. Long live the Quintet Chorus!"

And with this, the birds could be heard cheering throughout the wood, or were they having an extra choir practice that day.

Only they knew and now you do too, by reading this, their very first chorus adventure. And remember, the next time you go into a wood, think about what you could do to save the forest environment by protecting trees, plant life and animals (especially our feathered friends).

Your very own 'Quintet Chorus'!

The Quintet Chorus – A River Adventure

Join us in book two for the next exciting adventure of the Quintet Chorus.

There are huge problems in Willow River. Someone or something is poisoning the river animals and the chorus have a race against time to find out what is happening before it's too late.

About the Author

Ricky Elliott has worked in the world of Communications and Marketing for over 34 years. Recently retired, he bides his time between Movie Memorabilia buying, selling and collecting, Campanology (better known as ringing Church bells), Theatre going and Writing. The Quintet Chorus - A Woodland Adventure is his first novel. Ricky adds: "I think it is important for Young Children to learn more about the Environment in which they live. The Woods and Forests, the Rivers and the Land. And more importantly, how they can protect them for future Generations."